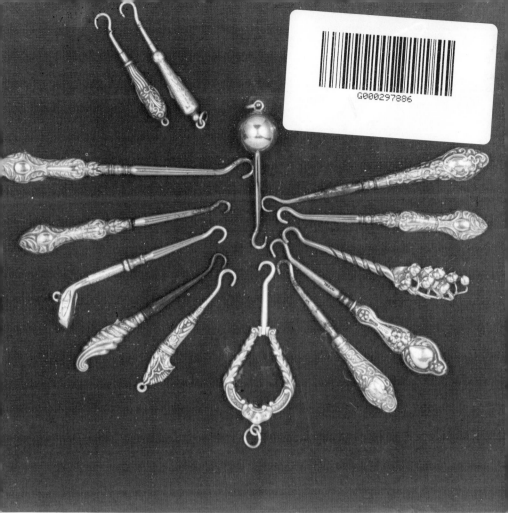

A selection of various silver-handled buttonhooks.

FASHION ACCESSORIES

Eleanor Johnson

Shire Publications Ltd

CONTENTS

Set in 10 point Times and printed in Great Britain by C. I. Thomas & Sons (Haverfordwest) Ltd, Press Buildings, Merlins Bridge, Haverfordwest.

A selection of hatpins.

(Anticlockwise from left) Silver-plated chatelaine, with finely cut centre clip (the hook to hang over the belt is behind this) and five elaborately decorated chains, carrying pincushion, pencil, scissors sheath, thimble bucket and notebook. Oval enamel box decorated in pale blue with birds at a bird bath and the words 'A Friend's Gift'. A small round porcelain box with painted lid and mirror inside the lid. Steel chatelaine, having three chains with pincushion, scissors in sheath and folding penknife. (Centre) Oval glass-topped metal ring box on feet.

INTRODUCTION

Fashion is primarily the result of the desire of the female to attract the male and to stand out among her contemporaries. This book is concerned with feminine fashion accessories of the period 1800 to 1914. The nineteenth century saw a much more rapid change in fashion than hitherto, although there were few original designs; most incorporated revivals of former styles, a trend which continues to the present day. The growth of new industrial processes, easier travel at home and abroad and migration from the country to the towns all played their part, making available and simplifying the purchase of a wider variety of fabrics and accessories. The Great Exhibition of 1851 had a profound influence, together with the increasing degree of prosperity of the middle classes, at its peak in the 1870s, the introduction of mass production, the appearance of the first department stores and the invention of the chain-stitch sewing machine.

In the early part of the century women were expected solely to be charming and attractive and to be occupied with the accepted feminine accomplishments, but as the years passed they revolted against this attitude and sought greater emancipation. Rigid customs and conventions were characteristic of society; ladies were judged by their appearance and the correct choice and manner of wearing clothes. Having much time on their hands, with servants taking care of the general running of the household, they could spend hours dressing and deliberating as to what to wear for each engagement or time of day. During the 1850s it became fashionable to drive or stroll in the public parks and gardens, showing off one's latest ensemble and commenting on or admiring those of other ladies in the parade.

ABOVE: *Ring stands. (From left) Transfer-printed white china, with convolvulus design; an arch with twigs. Silver, dated 1909, flower-shaped base with hooks on a central shaft. Silver, dated 1913; a moon with two hooks. Blue and white Jasper china. Silver, large flower-shaped base with central branch. Small silver, plain base with central twig. Turned wood, a central shaft with protruding sticks.*

BELOW: *Shoe horns. (Top) Silver handle with steel. (Bottom) Heavy silver handle with ivory.*

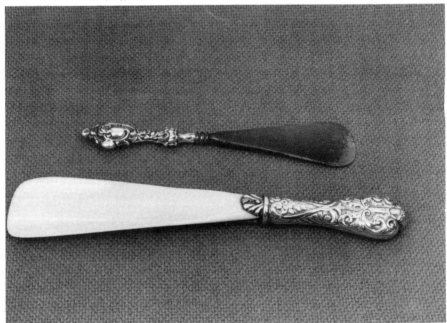

4

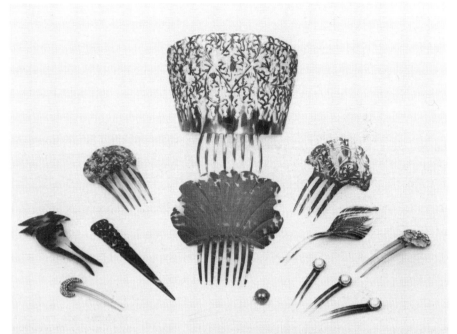

Hair combs. (From left, top row) Tortoiseshell with bird-shaped top. Imitation tortoiseshell with cut-out top. Large, elaborately cut, curved tortoiseshell. Imitation tortoiseshell with cut-out fan-shaped top. Tortoiseshell with cut steel facets. Blond tortoiseshell with hinged flower-shaped heading in enamel and paste jewels. (Bottom row) Two-pronged, blond tortoiseshell, with hinged crescent top set with cut steel. Tortoiseshell hair ornament. Large tortoiseshell comb. Three matching small imitation tortoiseshell pins with tops of imitation pearl surrounded with paste jewels. (Centre bottom) Two-pronged silver pin with round amethyst top.

ACCESSORIES ASSOCIATED
WITH THE TOILETTE

In the past as today the dressing table was most important to every self-respecting lady of fashion. There she would have her hand mirror, hairbrush, comb and clothes brush, together with a variety of small boxes, made of silver, ivory, wood, enamel on copper (most of these from Staffordshire makers), glass and English or French porcelain, and used to contain comfits, cachous (to sweeten the breath) or patches, which were used to accentuate beauty spots or conceal blemishes. Pots, usually concave inside for rouge or creams, would also be there.

Ring stands were a useful way of keeping safe precious, easily mislaid rings. They are usually formed like the branch of a tree or a hand with the fingers extended, fitted on a base, although others consist of a central rod or cone, with or without hooks. They were made in silver, ivory, wood, glass and china, including jasper ware, which has a matt finish to the raised pattern in white on a coloured ground.

Nail buffers and other manicure tools, together with shoe horns, are also collectable items. *Shoe horns* made of horn were and still are common, but others were fre-

5

quently of steel with decorated silver handles.

Hair combs of medium size, elaborately decorated, appeared during the classical revival of the early nineteenth century. They consisted of a number of gently curved prongs in tortoiseshell with a fancy heading, some hinged to enable the comb to lie flat against the head; they were often made of pressed-out metal, set with foil-backed paste jewels or semi-precious stones. Silver gilt, filigree and scrollwork patterns were popular at this time, while later the passion for eastern designs produced Islamic motifs, looped chains and imitation stones in coloured glass.

Cut steel was a popular type of decoration during the early and middle years of the century and it often ornaments tortoiseshell combs, together with pique, which is an inlay of small silver dots. More elaborate inlays, called pose, were also made using sheet gold or silver. Other ideas in the form of cameos, mosaic and coral were brought from abroad. During the 1860s it became fashionable to wear the hair in a chignon or coarse net, and large ornate combs fastened this to the main hair. When in 1861 the death of Prince Albert plunged Queen Victoria's court into mourning, black hair combs appeared to match the appropriate dress and jewellery. These were mostly made in real Whitby jet or in French jet, which is black glass cut and set to simulate the real thing. In the late nineteenth and early twentieth centuries silver combs became popular, some set with semi-precious stones or in the naturalistic and flowing art nouveau designs, initiated by William Morris and his followers.

Hair combs. (Top row from left) Silver with trefoil design. French jet in fan design. Engraved scrolled silver, dated 1897. (Bottom row) Silver with chrysoprase trefoil inset, dated 1905. Silver dated 1906 with thistle design.

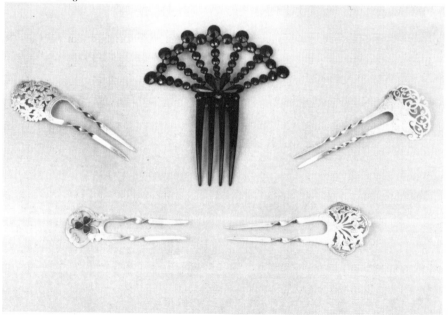

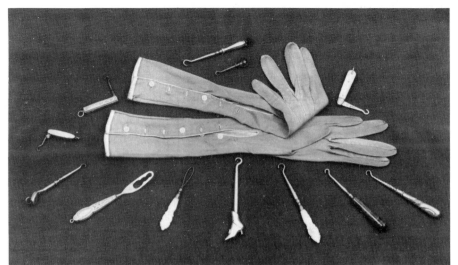

Buttonhooks, shown with long beige kid gloves fastened with tiny pearl buttons. (From top centre, clockwise) Plain silver-handled hook, with cut amethyst top. Tiny brass glove hook with round faceted amber-coloured stone. Mother-of-pearl handled folding silver hook, dated 1894. Sterling hook and handle. Hook with banded agate handle. Mother-of-pearl handled hook. Hook with silver-plated boot handle. Mother-of-pearl handled loop-shape hook, sometimes referred to as a spats hook (ladies also wore spats). Silver-handled loop shape, presumably for several sizes of button. Chatelaine silver glove hook, shaped like a golf club. Tiny folding chatelaine glove hook, decorated with turquoise enamel. Chatelaine steel hook folding into silver case.

BUTTONHOOKS

The word buttonhook is self-explanatory, but the reason for the widespread use of the buttonhook is not perhaps so obvious. Buttonhooks come in a variety of sizes, from a large heavy type 10 to 12 inches (250-310 mm) long, to as little as 1½ to 3 inches (40-60 mm) in length. In the nineteenth and early twentieth centuries women wore boots fastened at the side with a number of buttons. Stiff corsets made bending difficult, so a buttonhook was a valuable accessory. Medium-sized hooks could be used for footwear but were mostly used to fasten the numerous buttons on the bodices of dresses, from neck to hips, in the middle of the Victorian period. The smallest hooks and those which usually attract the majority of collectors are known as glove hooks and were used to fasten as many as fifteen buttons on the long gloves so fashionable from time to time during the Victorian and Edwardian eras.

The handles of the hooks frequently feature novelties, such as birds (especially owls), fish, animals, boots, or even Punch and Judy. They are made in a variety of materials, including silver, mother-of-pearl, jet, ivory, semi-precious stones – such as banded agate, coral or amethyst – enamel, coloured stones in round or faceted shapes, bone and wood. The working part of the hook is generally steel, to have the necessary strength, but some glove hooks have hallmarked silver handles and hooks. The hallmark gives the maker's initials, a date letter and a symbol for the assay office.

A number of cheap base-metal hooks were made to be given away or used as small change, advertising a particular product or shop. Some tiny hooks had a ring by which they could be attached to a chatelaine; this was a series of chains to carry needlework items or other useful necessities. Another type folded into a handle like a penknife or back into a pear-shaped handle.

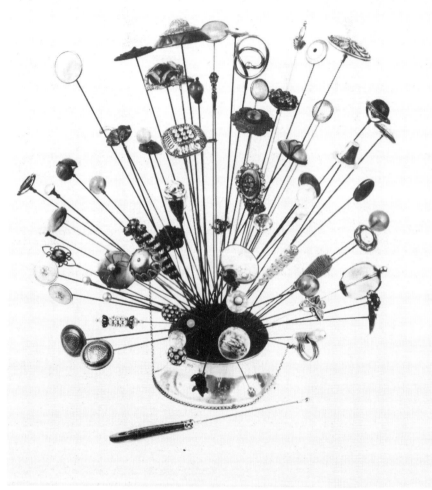

A selection of hatpins, including a pair of pale blue enamel on silver, several with hinged tops, a green marble butterfly set in a silver mount, a silver Welsh hat, a jade dog, a pair with painted Georgian figures on porcelain, a spider with a mauve stone body, an enamel pair with a basket of flowers in the centre, large pearl type with additional decorations, regimental buttons, one with a sword-hilt top, a lizard in brass with stones on its back, several in semi-precious stones (amethyst, serpentine and malachite), different-coloured glass tops, paste jewels, cameo, various metals, a pair of gilded pins linked with a chain, and, in front lying down, a hatpin with the protector in place. The pins are displayed in a large, weighted, silver-based blue velvet pincushion.

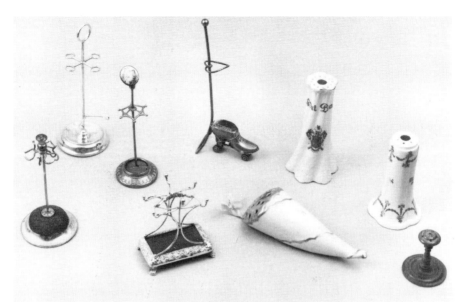

Hatpin stands. (From left) Hallmarked silver with blue velvet pincushion, having a citrine stone in the top and three heart shapes fixed to the central rod. Silver with four rings attached to the rod, topped with a lifting loop and with hooks for rings near the base. Brass with a hand-painted porcelain button top. An exceptionally delicate rectangular shape in silver, dated 1897, combined for hatpins and rings; a wire grid in the base holds the hatpins in place. A novelty stand in brass featuring a roller skate and boot with pincushion. A white china cornucopia shape open at the back, decorated in gold with a pink ribbon to hang on the dressing table. A souvenir crested china stand. Another decorated with garlands of flowers. A small wooden stand for short pins.

HATPINS AND HATPIN STANDS

The hatpin is a fashion accessory which only appeared when in the 1890s large flat hats placed on the top of the head became fashionable. Anyone who has handled one of these large pins, up to 12 inches (310 mm) long, which are the collector's items of today, can readily appreciate how lethal they could be. Injuries in crowds were not infrequent and they could be used as a defensive weapon.

The decorative tops vary in size from $\frac{1}{2}$ inch to $2\frac{1}{2}$ inches (15-60 mm) and are made of many materials, such as porcelain, including Japanese Satsuma, glass, silver, brass, tortoiseshell with pique, mother-of-pearl, ivory, enamel, paste, semi-precious stones, cut steel and jet. The designs themselves are colourful, ingenious and in infinite variety. Animal shapes, birds, butterflies, insects, buildings, fruit and flowers can all be found, together with button tops, both decorative and regimental.

Among the most sought-after hatpins are those with hallmarked silver tops made by Charles Horner of Halifax. They have the Chester mark and the initials *C H*. Another especially attractive type, usually about 6 to 8 inches (150-200 mm) long, comes in pairs and is decorated in enamels. Some hatpins have hinged tops to enable the pin to rest flat against the head.

The steel shafts of the pins vary in shape; some have a plain pointed end, some a flat bayonet-shaped point, and others a spiral shaft. Special protectors were patented which could be fitted when the hatpin was in place to prevent injury to

9

other people. Occasionally a pair of pins will be found which can be linked with a chain.

The most effective way to display a collection of hatpins is in a large weighted pincushion, but a great variety of stands and holders was made to display and store the pins. Stands were made in silver, silver plate and brass; they usually consist of a central rod fitted with a number of rings through which the pins could be placed and attached to a base plate fitted with a velvet-covered cushion. The top would be decorated in many different ways. China hatpin holders were usually vase-shaped, with a central hole surrounded with smaller holes. This type is often found in crested china souvenir designs, but there are also many other forms of decoration.

Glove stretchers. (Left, top to bottom) Wood, finely carved with dogs' heads. Silver-handled ivory. Brass. (Right, top to bottom) Fine-quality tortoiseshell with silver inlay. Steel stretchers with flower-decorated silver handles.

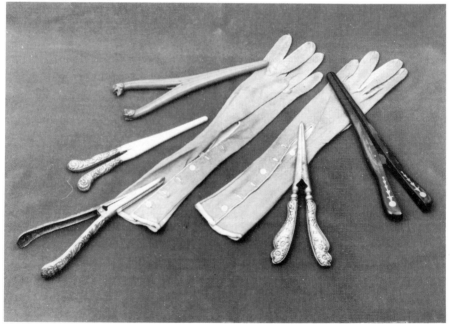

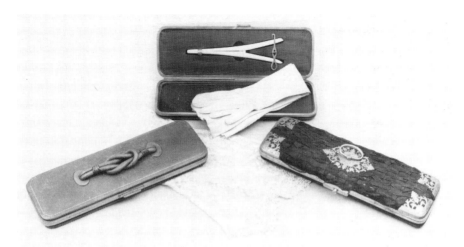

Glove boxes. (From left) Brown leather-covered concertina type case. A similar case open showing the glove stretchers and buttonhook; lined in green satin. Elaborate concertina case, covered in purple ruched silk, with brass centre mount, handle and corners. They are shown with a pair of long kid gloves and lace mittens.

GLOVE BOXES, GLOVE STRETCHERS AND POWDERING FLASKS

Throughout the nineteenth and early twentieth centuries gloves were an important dress accessory, being worn for daytime or evening in varying lengths. White kid was popular, and special boxes were used to keep them clean and neat. Some were simply a box in wood or papier-mache, the former painted or fabric-covered, but a more interesting type, usually covered in leather but occasionally in silk, was expanding, with concertina sides. Some have a fitted space inside the lid to hold glove stretchers and buttonhook.

Glove stretchers were used to restore the shape of the fingers of the gloves after washing, which made them wrinkled and stiff. They were made in boxwood, rosewood and ebony, but also in ivory, bone and brass. Wooden examples in Tartan and Mauchline souvenir wares are interesting. The Tartan type are decorated with coloured Tartan paper and the Mauchline are made in pale sycamore wood with a black transfer print of some place of interest or resort. The earliest type of stretcher had no spring, but later ones had this improvement. Another variety, made in steel with silver or ivory handles, is also fairly common. Some glove stretchers will be found in boxed sets with matching shoe horn and buttonhook.

The long gloves could be quite difficult to put on, and to simplify this it was usual to powder the insides. In order to apply the powder special glove-powdering flasks were made, usually in boxwood, ebony or ivory. They were shaped like a small bulbous wine bottle, the neck being screwed into the top of the bulb shape, which held the powder. The top of the long neck part was pierced with holes like a pepper pot, and some had a screw-on cap for this, though frequently these have been lost.

A selection of some of the more popular pieces of Georgian, Victorian and Edwardian jewellery, in-cluding chains, locket, brooches, watches, pendants, rings, bracelet and chain with chatelaine clip. The chain on the left is a Leontine, the long centre one is called a guard chain and the small watch on the bottom right inside a curve of the chain was to wear on the outside of a glove. The brooch bottom left is in pietra dura (coloured stones inlaid into black marble); the two centre left are (top) an ellip-tical one hand-painted on ivory in a gold mount and (below) a mourning brooch. Centre right is a Wedgwood cameo in a gilt metal surround. The chatelaine clip is decorated in fine enamel. The dainty pendant on the top right is in the art nouveau style, set with opals and garnets, and that on the top left is 15-carat gold set with pearls and amethysts. The butterfly brooch is set with turquoises, rubies and diamond chips. The small rectangular brooch top right is a mourning type with hair set in the centre and surrounded with amethysts.

Four rows of typical beads. (From left) Amber, round-shaped coral, ivory and cornelian, which were popular at the time of the Aesthetic Movement.

JEWELLERY

The primary purpose of jewellery is to make women appear more beautiful, and after the middle years of the nineteenth century they were eager to discover and wear the latest and most sensational. This desire was exploited to the full by artists, craftsmen and manufacturers, making use of new developments and innovations made possible by the introduction of new machines and methods of production. These led to there being more jewellery in the nineteenth century than in any previous era. Hitherto gold had been scarce and many pieces of jewellery were remade to meet changing fashions, but from this time onwards the supply became more plentiful, following the American gold rush, and that occurring subsequently in Australia. One reason for the increased demand was that jewellery was being more and more worn by the wives of the new industrialists, their husbands finding that this was an excellent way of advertising their own wealth and position.

The rapid succession of new fashions in clothes was matched by changes in popular jewellery. Not only gold, silver and precious gems were used, but semi-precious stones, ivory, coral, porcelain, enamels, seed pearls, horsehair, mosaics, tortoiseshell pique and Scottish stones. One delightful innovation was code jewels, the initial letter of the name of the stone making a word: for example, diamond, emerald, amethyst, ruby, emerald, sardonyx, topaz — *dearest*.

In the 1830s long chains were worn for muffs, watches and eyeglasses, while in 1875 they were used for lorgnettes. Another popular chain, the Leontine, was named after a well known actress. Earrings varied in size and shape and their design was influenced by hair styles; brooches ranged from small to large; rings and lockets, pendants and bracelets all had their place in changing styles at varying times. Mourning jewellery, which used locks of hair set into rings and brooches, had a great vogue, as did black materials of all kinds, especially jet and onyx. Insect motifs, such as butterflies, were popular, as were gold knobs and tassels, when the eastern influence was at its height. Cameos are typically Victorian together with art nouveau. Bar and named brooches were in great favour at the end of the nineteenth century and beginning of the twentieth.

13

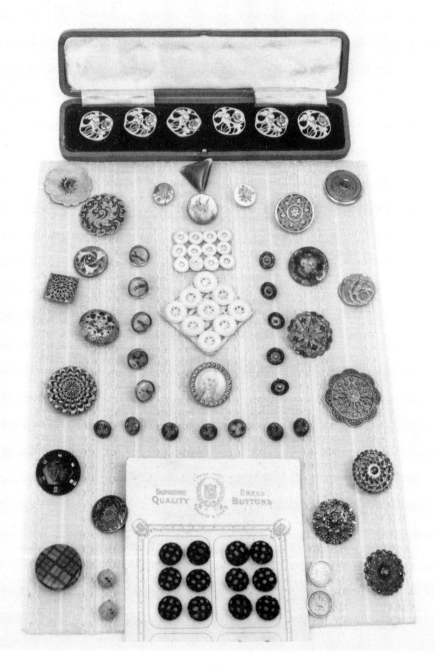

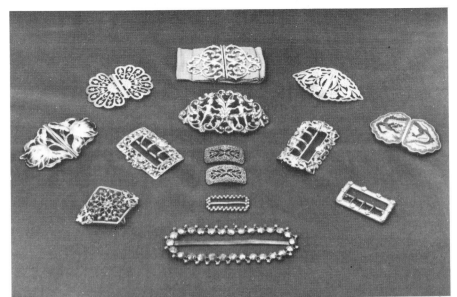

Buckles. (Top row from left) Art nouveau enamel on silver in tulip design, green and mauve. Neat fan-shaped design in silver. Another in silver with petersham belt. Elliptical flower design in silver made in Birmingham. Cloisonne enamel (the design is made in brass wire and the enamel applied inside). (Inner row) Cut steel and brass shoe buckle. Fine silver belt buckle dated 1895. Silver with figures and leaves. Another silver belt buckle. One with turquoises set in gilt metal. (Centre, top to bottom) A pair of cut steel shoe buckles and a small and a large cut steel example.

BUTTONS AND BUCKLES

Buttons have been used throughout history as a fastening for garments, but it was not until the nineteenth century that they came into their own as a complement to women's fashions and were to proliferate in a manner hitherto unseen. The demand for buttons in this period grew, and the availability of new materials and new industrial processes made it possible to produce an infinite variety of more decorative buttons than had ever been seen before.

For much of this period cut steel was popular; many designs were made in stamped-out metal, including mirror backs, in which the raised perforated top covers a reflective backing. Most buttons of this type were made in two pieces: a separate top fitted to a base, with a looped shank for sewing on to the garment. Enamel buttons

OPPOSITE: *A selection of buttons on a sampler, with a boxed set of silver art nouveau style, dated 1909. (Left, top to bottom) Two heavy metal Paris backs decorated in enamel with brass scrolls. Paris back buttons are much sought after by collectors; they were made in Paris and have the initials of the maker. A lily pattern metal and enamel button. A square mirror back. A raised metal two-piece. A large round mirror back. A part set of waistcoat buttons featuring a print of golfers. A black button with lustre decoration. Stamped-out brass. One in painted Tartan. Two small stone buttons. (Centre, top to bottom) Triangular green porcelain type called Ruskin. Two Japanese Satsuma in porcelain, with designs of irises, and a hand-painted porcelain one below. Two original cards of Dorset cartwheel buttons, which were handmade in thread. A lithograph button, the print surrounded with cut steel. Seven small dress buttons. Part of an original card of fabric-covered buttons. (Right, top to bottom) A pair of two-piece Paris backs. Five matching waistcoat buttons. Dark blue enamel with flower design. A brass art nouveau design. Metal and enamel. Pierced brass with scalloped edge. Three in cut steel. Two buttons made from threepenny pieces.*

15

were both beautiful and popular, as were those in hallmarked silver, art nouveau designs being in demand with collectors today. Mother-of-pearl and glass buttons were plentiful, the most interesting of the latter being paperweight buttons, which resemble miniature versions of the large desk item. After the death of the Prince Consort black buttons were made in fabric and black glass, some of these relieved by lustre decoration. Lithograph buttons are another interesting collector's item; these have a small portrait or subject print set in a metal mount under glass or celluloid, sometimes surrounded by facets in cut steel or paste jewels. In the latter part of the Victorian period small sets of buttons were made, called the 'Downfall of Man', featuring wine, women and song. A similar type pictured sports and animals. Small waistcoat and dress buttons in black and numerous other varied designs are the most common extant from this time, but occasionally one finds hand-painted porcelain, Satsuma, hardstone, tortoiseshell pique or ivory buttons.

Buckles for shoes and belts were also made in variety throughout this period, featuring most of the materials used for other items. Hallmarked silver examples are among the most desirable, and today many of these are worn by the nursing profession. They are frequently given as a congratulatory gift to a young nurse who has achieved State Registration.

SKIRT LIFTERS

Many people seeing these strange items puzzle over their purpose, but once their use is revealed they give a fascinating glimpse into the life of a past age. During most of the nineteenth century drainage was haphazard and uncollected garbage was thrown out into unswept streets that in many places were not yet macadam surfaced, thus costly full-skirted long dresses were easily soiled. Many ladies drove in a carriage or might use the services of a crossing sweeper, who had to be given a tip. In the last quarter of the century skirt lifters, also known as pages, were produced. They were ingenious devices looking rather like a pair of strange scissors; two pivoted arms ending in cushioned circles could be locked by a contrivance at the top between the two arms and operated by a cord suspended from the waist. A corner of the skirt hem was placed between the discs, which were then locked tight, and a pull on the cord lifted the skirt free of the ground. The locking devices were decorated in a variety of ways; hands, butterflies, horseshoes, and other scrolled designs were popular. The clips were always made in non-precious metals, usually brass or plated. Some models had a matching miniature version attached and there were a number of different patent styles. Some types turn up in pairs and it is possible that these could have been used when cycling.

PARASOLS

Although parasols have been known throughout history as a protection from the sun, it was during the nineteenth century, when ladies became particularly concerned to preserve their delicate complexions, that this accessory enjoyed much more widespread popularity; in addition, however, their potential as an aid to flirtation was quickly appreciated by fashionable women.

The early examples of parasols were small and dainty, covered in lightweight fabrics, such as lace or silk, and trimmed with silk fringes. The sticks were long, topped by small handles made of ivory, wood or mother-of-pearl. One popular shape was the pagoda, and a special carriage parasol was evolved, with a handle in two hinged parts, having a deep ring which could be slid up to secure the hinged area.

As fashions changed in the second half of the century, the small styles were superseded by larger types, more elaborately trimmed and with large china, wood or crystal handles. As the century progressed, they were often covered to match the outfit and later still were covered in much heavier, more gaudily coloured materials.

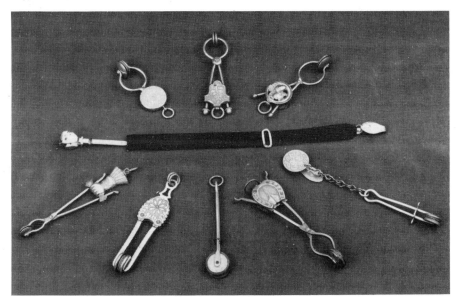

ABOVE: *Skirt lifters. (Top row from left) Patent silver metal, decorated with flowers, with engraved initials S & W on round centre plate, called Knights Eclipse, opened by turning round plate clockwise. Brass shield shape decorated with fern leaf. Silver metal, circular locking plate decorated with acorns. (Centre) Black moire ribbon with steel hook and clip. (Bottom row from left) Brass decorated with hand and gauntlet. Plated Walton and Shaw's patent, with initials MB on reverse, plate decorated with engraved pattern; opens by moving centre top handle clockwise. Simple type with padded cushions and slide-up ring. Brass decorated with horseshoe plate. Simple type with chain and clip; may have been used for cycling.*
BELOW: *Two folding carriage parasols. (Left) Black and gold silk with matching fringe, wooden handle showing folding mechanism. (Right) Cream embroidered silk cover lined with cream silk and with silk fringe, the wooden handle fully extended.*

17

ABOVE: *Scent bottles. (Lower ring from left) Three small late nineteenth-century Venetian glass bottles made for the tourist trade, each with original stoppers, one green, one white with coloured decoration, and one small dark green shaped like a die. Dark red enamel torpedo shape decorated with a figure, and with flowers on the hinged lid, and with silver gilt mounts. Porcelain egg with silver bird head for top. Silver egg shape with finely chased decoration. Acorn shape in deep ruby glass, with gilt shell. Two more in Venetian glass. A small bottle in moulded glass with matching stopper. (Inner ring from left) Deep blue glass double-ended type with silver mounts and lids. Small cylindrical cut glass with silver screw top. Flat multicoloured and silvered glass with tight fitting stopper, Italian, nineteenth and twentieth centuries. Flat silver chatelaine bottle. Porcelain with transfer print of Prestatyn pier and silver top. Deep ruby glass with finely chased hinged silver top. Clear glass lined with deep blue, decorated with gold stars and having hinged gold top. (Top centre) Heavy round cut glass dressing-table cologne bottle with silver screw top. (Below this) Square clear glass bottle with lithograph print set in lid.*
BELOW: *(Top row from left) Scent bottle holder in fine tortoiseshell pique, opened by press button catch, and having a glass bottle with stopper inside. Silver-handled nail buffer. Tortoiseshell pique necessaire containing scent bottle and manicure tools. (Bottom row) Small purse mirror in whalebone, Georgian. Silver comb case. Miniature silver mirror with ring to hang on chatelaine.*

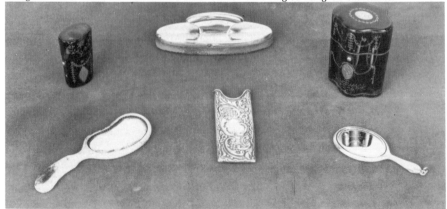

A very fine example of a silver vinaigrette, with the original gilded grille in elaborate scrollwork. The base and lid are finely engraved.

SCENT BOTTLES

Perfume has a long and fascinating history, being used on the person as well as having a ritual and religious significance since very early times. It has always been a luxury commodity and early containers were made in costly materials to be worthy of their expensive contents. Sweet-scented substances were used in creams and ointments for use on the skin, produced in solid form to be carried in pomanders and used for smelling salts and in concentrated form or in toilet waters. It is the specific use which produces the variety of containers which enchant present-day collectors. In modern times the sole use of perfume is to make women more attractive, but in former days it was also believed that it could prevent infection.

As the nineteenth century progressed, the growth of industrialism brought greater affluence to a wider range of the population, and happily for the present-day collector the production of scent bottles multiplied. As in other fields, ingenuity and imagination in design together with the use of a wide range of materials produced an extensive choice.

The very nature of scent has governed the design of containers. The fact that it is so volatile necessitates a tightly fitting lid, and protection from strong light is sometimes important to prevent deterioration.

Scent bottles were made of porcelain, both of English and continental origin, glass, such as Stourbridge, Bristol and Nailsea, silver, brass, enamel, hardstones, ivory and fruit stones. Wood was used to make containers for plain glass bottles. A large number of perfume bottles were made of glass in various forms; some were plain, others coloured, others still in overlay (in which the colour is fused over clear glass and a design then cut with a wheel). Opaline glass, cameo, Venetian, aventurine, enamelled and trailed patterns are also found. Large toilet water bottles are plentiful, for cologne or lavender water; these are often in cut glass with silver tops. Small bottles to carry in the pocket or reticule are numerous, and fairly plentiful are the double-ended type, usually in deep blue, red or green. These consist of two bottles fused together at the base, mostly round or oc-

19

tagonal, and have brass, silver-plated or silver tops; one of these is hinged and conceals a small glass stopper; the other is a screw top with a patent seal inside the lid. One final type of glass container is a slender cylindrical or flat-sided tube, known as Oxford Lavender, and intended as a throw-away type.

Some of the small bottles had a short chain so that they could be worn suspended on a longer chain or on a chatelaine clip. From 1820 to 1830 these were fashionable, while in the next decade smelling bottles were worn on a hook at the waist. From

1850 to 1860 scent bottles worn in this way were replaced by posies.

A few very fine necessaires or bottle containers in tortoiseshell pique can be found, but these have become expensive if perfect.

Under this heading may be mentioned vinaigrettes or smelling boxes. These are very small gold or silver boxes, engraved or engine-turned, having a perforated grille inside, which covers a sponge soaked in aromatic vinegar. The inside of the box is heavily gilded to prevent corrosion, and the lid fits tightly to avoid evaporation.

Purses. (Top row from left) Round leather purse with flat metal frame picturing the Eiffel Tower. Double-ended gold velvet with snap fastenings. Round flat concertina shape in leather with owl's face decoration. (Centre row) Leather in four sections with expanding metal top held closed by a fitting lid. Wooden Mauchline example with transfer print of the Hotel de Beuzeval. Small brass coin purse, of the type possibly used to carry coins for the church collection. Brass with painted decoration. Leather-covered convex shape with metal initial C. (Bottom row) Small early nineteenth-century steel mesh. Steel beaded with silver-plated mounts set with turquoises and with chain. Small handmade beaded purse, black with coloured flowers, having gilt metal mounts.

Purses. (Top row from left) Tortoiseshell with inlaid silver panel and brass mounts. Dark blue knitted miser's purse decorated with steel beads and silver rings. Tortoiseshell with blond tortoiseshell initial M and blue silk compartments inside. (Middle row) Beautiful silver chatelaine purse dated 1913, elaborately engraved, shaped and opening like a purse with a flap. Small round coin purse open to show inner blue silk compartments. Silver mesh purse, with silver mounts and chain. Small coin type, same as the left-hand model, but closed to show lithograph print of Crystal Palace. Silver chatelaine purse with ring and chain, made in Birmingham in 1906, the front panel engraved with initials and having a clip fastening. (Bottom row) Gilt metal purse with five inset lithograph prints of the Paris Exhibition, opening to reveal compartments. Heavy crocheted blue silk miser's purse decorated with steel beads and shown with nineteenth-century coins all belonging to the original owner. Steel and mother-of-pearl with patent fastening.

PURSES

Practically every late twentieth-century woman would feel lost without her handbag, that valuable accessory in which she carries all the paraphernalia seemingly indispensable to her daily life. It was, however, not until 1880 that the first leather handbags were made and became popular. Earlier in the century fashions in clothes dictated the means of carrying the items necessary to the comfort and convenience of a lady. When skirts were full, they concealed pockets made as part of the dress or tied on separately, but when skirts were slim and clinging, some other form had to be used. This was when the reticule (a corruption of the word 'ridicule') was popularised. It could be made as a fabric Dorothy bag closed with a drawstring or be a beaded bag sometimes hung from the waist by a chatelaine hook. There is a fascinating variety of purses in all shapes, styles and sizes from the Victorian and Edwardian periods to tempt the collector.

Some of the early purses were decorated with cut steel beads, which were very fashionable. These were followed by miser's purses, these being generally a slim sausage shape, knitted or crocheted in silk and also decorated with beads. Two rings could be slid along to hold the coins in each end away from the central slit. Very tiny purses in brass, mother-of-pearl, tortoiseshell and silver, some to hang from a chain on a chatelaine hook, were made to carry a few coins, perhaps for the church collection. Purses were made in every kind of material and similarly the designs and sizes are infinitely varied.

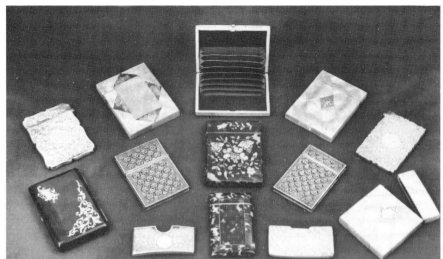

ABOVE: *Card cases. (Top row from left) Finely engraved example in silver. Cameo carved mother-of-pearl with abalone triangles, hinged top. Mother-of-pearl, side fastening type, open to show typical inside compartments. Mother-of-pearl with engraved silver diamond-shaped plate inlaid. Another fine silver case dated 1894. (Centre row) Tortoiseshell with silver decoration, side opening, having ivory notepad and pencil inside. Silver gilt filigree, about 1820-30, with slide-off top. Very attractive tortoiseshell inlaid with mother-of-pearl flower design, having hinged lid. Silver filigree, also early nineteenth century. Mother-of-pearl, open to show hinged top opening. (Bottom row) Two gentlemen's engraved silver card cases, dated 1898 and 1903, flanking an early nineteenth-century smaller tortoiseshell case with silver pique.*

BELOW: *Card cases. (Top row from left) A packet of visiting cards for mourning. An open leather-covered case. Another open case, which has plain ivory covers, showing the ivory pencil and loops for closing. (Bottom row) Card case in ivory inlaid with steel and abalone shell, over wood. Deeply carved sandalwood with similar decoration; slide-off lid. Deep purple fabric-covered card, with embroidered centre panel and corners, and opening in unusual fashion.*

22

Notebooks. (Outer ring from left) Tiny mother-of-pearl covered carnet-de-bal, with silver panel and metal holder for pencil. Green Tartan-covered paper notebook with metal fastening. Red plush-covered book with inset lithograph print of Osborne House. Embroidered purple velvet dated 1843. Mauchline ware example with a transfer print of Bournemouth, having red leather spine and pencil. Paper dance programme, listing waltz, lancers, galop and quadrille, with space opposite for partners' names, the names being actually written in pencil. (Centre top) Tiny silver-covered almanac in art nouveau design, with a calendar for 1918 printed by Brights of Bournemouth inside. Mother-of-pearl and abalone covered notebook with metal fastening complete with pencil. (Centre below) Silver covers enclosing ivory leaves, made in 1898, with loop to hang on chatelaine. Card dance programme, similar to the open example, but for the Bath Assembly Rooms on Thursday 10th January 1884. All are displayed on a pale green pure silk shawl with typical embroidery and silk fringe.

CARD CASES AND NOTEBOOKS

Card cases were used throughout the nineteenth century and well into the twentieth, but the majority to be found today date from 1850 onwards, when production was at its height. Members of upper-class society spent the season in London and the remainder of the year in the country, visiting or entertaining. Calling and leaving cards was an important activity occupying much of the time of leisured ladies. It was considered essential to make one's way in society, and there was the overriding consideration of marrying one's sons and daughters in the right quarters. To be successful in this aim meant following the correct codes of behaviour and being known in the right company. Books on eti-

quette for the period give precise instructions for all occasions on all aspects of calling and leaving cards. The cards had to be of a specified size for ladies and gentlemen, thus accounting for the difference in the size of the card cases, those for ladies being larger. The cards had to be printed in a carefully prescribed way, and for mourning edged with a black band of regulation width.

Card cases were made in a wide variety of materials including hallmarked silver, but these have now become expensive. Mother-of-pearl and tortoiseshell, sometimes with silver inlays, were popular, and often abalone shell was incorporated, in a pattern of diamond-shaped panes.

Cameo carving or fretted designs in mother-of-pearl are particularly attractive. Plain or carved ivory, papier-mache and lacquer decorated with mother-of-pearl inlay or painted, wood in souvenir Tunbridge, Tartan or Mauchline ware or deeply carved, for instance in sandalwood, which also had inlays of shell, steel and ivory, are quite common, as also are others in marquetry, bois durci (a composition made to look like wood), leather-covered card, straw work and early synthetics.

A number of these were imported from abroad and they remind us that the Victorian period saw the spread of the British Empire. Naturally, while living or staying abroad, British subjects carried on their normal customs, so they would use card cases made in local styles and materials.

Notebooks are another attractive type of collectable accessory, some having paper leaves and some ivory leaves. They were made in many sizes and materials, often being closed by a pencil slipped through loops. The most charming are those having mother-of-pearl, ivory or elaborately decorated silver or silver-plated covers enclosing the ivory leaves. Occasionally these leaves are printed with the days of the week. Sometimes the cover has the words *carnet-de-bal* inscribed on it; this was a dance programme on which to write the names of one's partners for the individual dances at a ball.

FANS

The earliest use of the fan was simply as a cooling aid, but as civilisation developed it came to have a much more complex ritual significance, especially in the Far East, as well as being useful, and ultimately it acquired social importance. The highest forms of art and craftsmanship were employed in making such a highly esteemed accessory.

When in town or the country, the leisured upper and middle classes indulged in frequent evening activities; Jane Austen's novel *Sense and Sensibility* gives a vivid picture of this. At dances and balls the atmosphere in crowded rooms could be hot and stuffy, which, in addition to the discomfort of constricting and uncomfortable clothes, must have made a fan a comfort indeed. It was, however, also a social attribute, requiring graceful movement of the hands and being capable of artful and eloquent use to convey emotions. In an age when the young were never allowed to meet alone, words and glances could be exchanged under its cover, and a complex language of the fan was developed. To touch the fan with the tip of the finger meant 'I wish to speak to you'. Fans became fashionable in an era when it was socially acceptable to be affected and if a lady was attending a rather risqué play she could make good use of a type of fan called Lorgnette. This had small holes in some of the sticks, covered with net or glass, through which she could observe all that was going on, while apparently shielding her eyes.

There are two main types of fan; rigid and folding. The first had a single piece of shaped material attached to a central stick. This material might be wood or papier-mache with mother-of-pearl or painted decoration, or feathers or fabric decorated with painting or embroidery. This type was popular from 1840 onwards. Folding fans are made up of two outer guards and a number of sticks in between opening out into a semicircle, and all held together by a pinion to which may be attached a finger ring. This type are covered with a single leaf decorated in a variety of ways, painted or embroidered with sequins, and made of paper, fabric, lace or very fine skin. One type of folding fan is called Brisé; this has small pieces of ribbon inserted through slots in the sticks and guards linking them together. Another type, the Cockade, unfolds from inside a double handle.

France was the chief centre for the manufacture of fans, although there were English makers. The name of Duvelleroy became famous in Britain after the Great Exhibition of 1851.

In the latter part of the nineteenth century when fans had become very large after varying in size at different periods, according to the dictates of fashion, the folding type were formed of large ostrich feathers or covered in much heavier materials.

Fans. (Top) Folding fan with blond tortoiseshell sticks, leaf of net with applique lace and bobbin lace trimming; metal pinion, and initials AC on guard; late Victorian. Cantonese Mandarin fan in original lacquer box lined with red paper painted with a Chinese design; the fan has gold decorated sticks and guards and a painted leaf showing Chinese figures, each one with a tiny painted ivory face. (Centre) Folding fan with gold decorated mother-of-pearl sticks and guards; the paper leaf painted with a design of figures, the whole mounted on very fine skin (known as chicken skin). The sticks and guards have a design of birds, flowers and leaves in gold; about 1850. (Bottom left) Screen fan, one of a pair, made in papier-mache inlaid with mother-of-pearl, with a design of a church in moonlight; a gilded wood handle; also about 1850. (Bottom right) Regency fan with blond tortoiseshell sticks and guards, with gilded decoration; finger ring attached; the leaf is of green silk and net, with gilt flower and leaf spangled decoration.

POSY HOLDERS

These charming Victorian accessories have now become scarce and expensive. They were carried in the hand and were usually funnel-shaped and made in deeply cut gold, silver or pinchbeck (a cheap substitute for gold, made from zinc and copper and named after Christopher Pinchbeck, who invented it in the early eighteenth century). Sometimes they had mother-of-pearl handles. A complete specimen should have a pin to secure the posy and a ring on a chain to be looped on the finger while dancing. Posies were not simply carried to be attractive, but also to counter the results of poor standards of personal hygiene in hot and crowded ballrooms. Between 1830 and 1840 artificial flowers were popular, and at this time smelling bottles were carried hung on a hook at the waist.

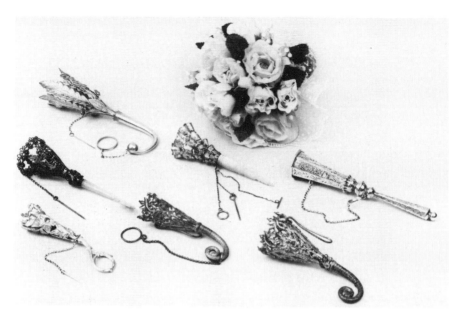

ABOVE: *Posy holders, displayed with a typical posy. (Top row slanting from left to right) Continental silver, leaves forming a funnel which can be opened out wider or closed as shown, complete with pin to secure the posy and a finger ring. Elaborate gilt metal in a frilled design with a mother-of-pearl handle, ring and pins. Very fine engraved continental silver example. (Centre row) Floral gilt metal design with curved mother-of-pearl handle and pin. Smaller gilt metal with curved handle and ring. Another in gilt metal, probably pinchbeck, with curved handle and a hook by which the holder could be fastened over the belt. (Bottom left) Small continental silver type with pin and integral finger ring as the handle.*

BELOW: *Lorgnettes. (Left) Folding tortoiseshell-handled example, held closed with a metal fastener. (Right) Rigid eyepieces fold straight down into imitation tortoiseshell handle.*

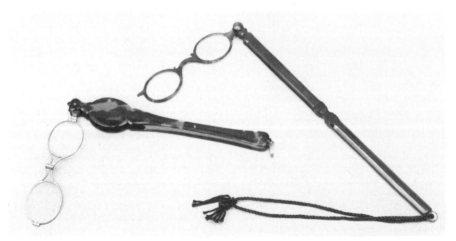

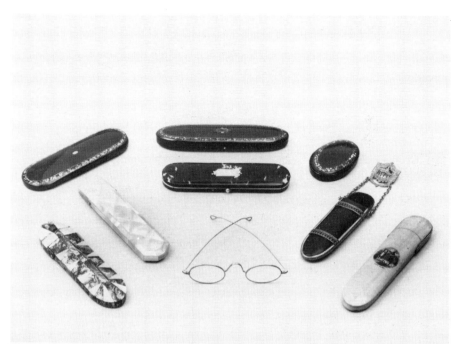

Spectacle cases. (Top row from left) Three examples in papier-mache inlaid with mother-of-pearl; elongated oval, elliptical, and small oval, all lined in blue silk; one with the optician's name in gilt lettering, all opening at the side. (Centre) A fine example in tortoiseshell with a silver plate for a name, lined in rose pink velvet. (Bottom left) A hinged-top case made in mother-of-pearl and abalone shell in shaped panes. Another in mother-of-pearl, also with forward opening hinged top. (Right) Metal and leather chatelaine type holder. Mauchline example with print of the Laxey Wheel, also with top opening towards the print. Shown with a typical pair of gold-rimmed spectacles.

SPECTACLE CASES AND GLASSES

Bygone spectacles were somewhat different in style to the modern version, usually with flattened oval-shaped lenses with or without sidepieces and occasionally folding. These slipped into fairly slim cases shaped according to the type, several examples being illustrated in the photograph.

At the end of the 1870s lorgnettes were popular, being worn on long chains. These are sometimes straight and flat and sometimes folding, made in silver, gold, pinchbeck, tortoiseshell with or without piqué, and also in synthetic tortoiseshell, mostly with long handles.

From 1810 to 1820 eyeglasses were fashionable, being worn on a ribbon or chain round the neck. They are sometimes known as quizzing glasses.

One occasionally finds very small gold hooked pins by which a glass or spectacles could be attached to the dress.

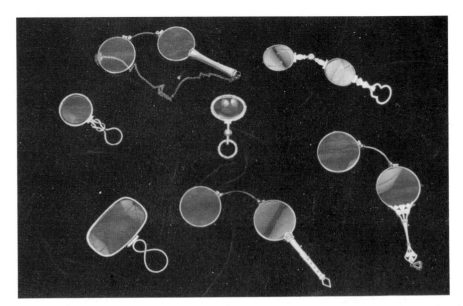

ABOVE: *Folding lorgnettes and quizzing glasses. (Top from left) Gold glass with round lens and reef knot handle. Folding lorgnette with smoky pearl handle and chain. 9-carat gold chased frame glass with oval lens. Silver folding lorgnette with ring to attach to ribbon or chain. (Bottom) Gold-framed rectangular-shaped glass with figure of eight handle. Continental silver folding lorgnette. 9-carat gold folding lorgnette with elegant trefoil decorated handle.*

BELOW: *Toothpick boxes and toothpicks. (Top) Fine oval ivory toothpick box with gold mounts and plaited hair inset under glass in lid; lined in green silk with mirror in lid; Regency. (Bottom row from left) Brass toothpick box in reeded design, lined in green velvet with metal bar to hold toothpicks inside; ring to attach to chain or chatelaine and very strong spring to close. Toothpick fitted into unscrewing top of. ivory container decorated with gold pique; early nineteenth-century. Toothpick retracting by screwing action into gold pencil-like container with cairngorm stone set into the top.*

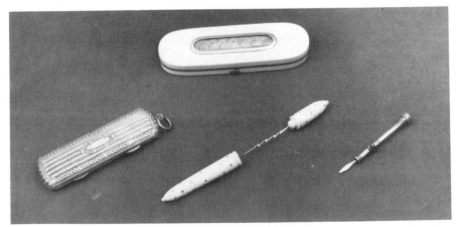

28

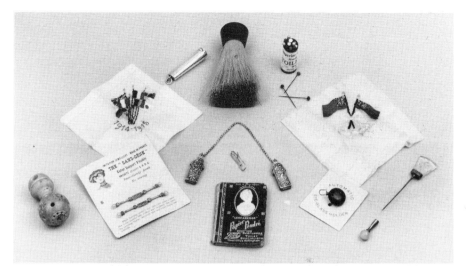

A collection of fashion-related items: a pomander in vegetable ivory (the fruit of a tree, the corozo nut); a pair of Edwardian collar stiffeners; two First World War handkerchiefs; a silver container for a cigarette holder; a bonnet brush; a packet of pins; a pair of cape fasteners with chain; an eyeglass hook; Boots 'Papier Poudre'; an automatic eyeglass holder; a small hatpin in intaglio design and a hatpin protector.

CONCLUSION

To the items already described can be added a number of other interesting accessories. Among these are muff warmers, which are miniature containers in copper or stoneware shaped like a hot water bottle. Toothpick cases in ivory with varied decoration, or in brass or pinchbeck, are particularly desirable items that are now scarce and expensive. Opera glasses, with or without handles and some in luxury materials, are quite common. Numerous other items of less monetary value, but nonetheless fascinating to the collector, can be discovered and give an insight into the life of former times. Most of the accessories described in this album can be found from time to time in antique shops, antique fairs and markets.

The comparative peace and security of the Edwardian period with its greater freedom and relaxation, after the rigidity and conformism of the Victorian era, were completely lost in the changes which followed the First World War. A new and more utilitarian age was ushered in, which has continued until the jeans and T-shirts fashion of the present day. However, there has been in the past two decades a great revival of interest in the everyday things of the past, and perhaps not a little nostalgia for a more romantic and elegant age. This is satisfied in many people by their deep and rewarding interest in collecting bygones from an era unknown to them except through books, television, pictures and maybe a grandmother's memory. It is hoped that this book will help those already in the ranks of collectors and perhaps stimulate others to begin.

29

Fine-quality porcelain scent bottle decorated with painted figure.

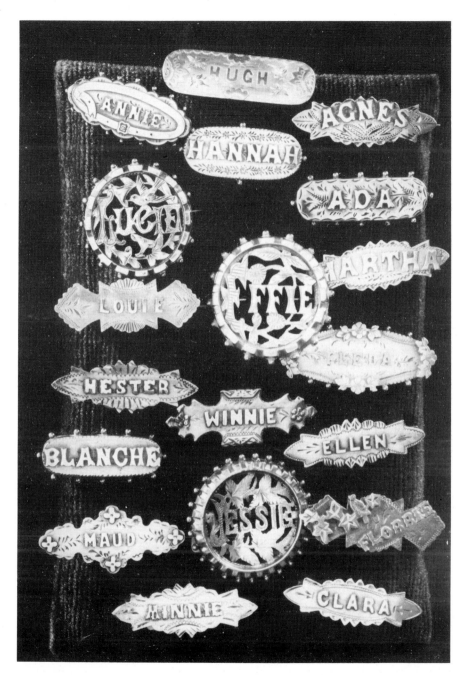

A selection of silver named brooches.

FURTHER READING

Armstrong, Nancy. *A Collector's History of Fans*. London, 1974.
Baker, Lillian. *The Collector's Encyclopaedia of Hatpins and Hatpin Holders*. Collector Books, Kentucky, USA, 1976.
Hill, Hamilton and Bucknell, Peter A. *The Evolution of Fashion*. Batsford, 1967.
Hinks, Peter. *Nineteenth Century Jewellery*. Faber and Faber, 1975.
Launert, Edmund. *Scent and Scent Bottles*. Barrie and Jenkins, 1974.
Peacock, Primrose. *Buttons for the Collector*. David and Charles, 1972.
Peacock, Primrose. *Discovering Old Buttons*. Shire Publications, 1978.
Scott, Christopher and Amoret. *Collecting Bygones*. Max Parrish, 1964.

PLACES TO VISIT

Blaise Castle House Museum, Henbury, Bristol. Telephone: Bristol (0272) 625378.
Cecil Higgins Art Gallery, Castle Close, The Embankment, Bedford. Telephone: Bedford (0234) 211222.
Chertsey Museum, The Cedars, Windsor Street, Chertsey, Surrey. Telephone: Chertsey (093 28) 65764.
Churchill Gardens Museum, Venn's Lane, Hereford. Telephone: Hereford (0432) 67409.
Hereford and Worcester County Museum, Hartlebury Castle, Hartlebury, Kidderminster. Telephone: Hartlebury (029 96) 416.
Killerton House (National Trust), near Exeter, Devon. Telephone: Hele (039 288) 345. (A superb collection of costume displayed in realistic settings in the various rooms).
Museum of Costume, Assembly Rooms, Alfred Street, Bath. Telephone: Bath (0225) 28411.
Museum of London, London Wall, London EC2. Telephone: 01-600 3699.

ACKNOWLEDGEMENTS

My thanks go to the following for the loan of items for the photographs and for other assistance: Pamela Broadfoot, Nigel Daniell, Floriat of Beaminster, Patricia Gyldard, Ann Lingard, Dora and Gerald James, Pat and Graham Smith, M. Spiller and Judith Pollitt of Times Past, Pershore. I am also grateful to P. Isbell and George Mell for the loan of photographs (pages 1, 2, 30 and 31) and to Joyce Mell for the silver brooches in the photograph on page 31. The other photographs are by Michael Bass, Reed Photography, Tring.